Poe's The Raven

facsimile reproduction of
1884 folio, illustrated by

Gustave Doré

Introduction by
DAN MALAN
Author of comprehensive reference work:
GUSTAVE DORÉ - *Adrift on Dreams of Splendor*

1996

Malan Classical Enterprises
St. Louis, MO

ISBN 0-9631135-3-4

Published by   Malan Classical Enterprises
                      7519 Lindbergh Dr.
                      St. Louis, MO 63117-2135
                      Phone: (314) 781-2319
                      FAX: (314) 781-0699

Edgar Allan Poe   (1809-1849) U.S. Author, Poet, and Journalist
Gustave Doré   (1832-1883) French Illustrator, Painter, and Sculptor
Dan Malan   (1951-   )

ILLUSTRATIONS: All of the illustrations reproduced herein are now in the public domain and may be photocopied at will, except for the illustration by Bill Elder (© 1954 E.C.Comics / William Gaines) and the illustration by Gahan Wilson (© 1990 Berkley / First Publishing).

   Shown here is the cover design on the decorative box which held the American edition of the 1884 Doré folio of *Poe's The Raven*.

TABLE OF CONTENTS

Life of Gustave Doré, by Dan Malan

While it may be subjective to assert that Gustave Doré was the greatest illustrator who ever lived, any objective standard used to judge such a claim yields the same conclusion. No other illustrator ever came close to his 10,000 engravings, including 1,500 full-page folio engravings. No other illustrator ever came close to the 3,000 book editions which contain his illustrations. And no one has ever come close to the range of literary classics he brought to life through visual imagery. Doré set the standard for the artistic expression of literary classics, such as:

Edmond About: *King of the Mountains*
Hans Christian Andersen: *The Nightingale*
Ludovico Ariosto: *Orlando Furioso*
Honore de Balzac: *Droll Stories*
Pierre-Jean de Beranger: *Poems*
The Bible (including *The Apocrypha*)
Lord Byron: *Complete Works*
Miguel de Cervantes: *Don Quixote*
Vicomte de Chateaubriand: *Atala*
Sam.T.Coleridge:*Rime of the Ancient Mariner*
Dante Alighieri: *The Divine Comedy*
Charles Dickens: *A Christmas Carol*
Alexandre Dumas: *Jehu's Companions*
Paul Feval: *Gold Hunters*
Antoine Galland: *Arabian Nights*
Theophile Gautier: *Captain Fracasse*
Thomas Hood: *Poems*
Victor Hugo: *Hunchback of Notre Dame*
              Toilers of the Sea
Jean de LaFontaine: *Fables* (= Aesop)
Henry Wadsworth Longfellow: *Poems*
John Milton: *Paradise Lost*
Michel de Montaigne: *Essays*
Sir Thomas Moore: *The Epicurean*
Charles Perrault: *Fairy Tales* (= Grimm)
Edgar Allan Poe: *The Raven*
Francois Rabelais: *Gargantua & Pantagruel*
Rudolph Eric Raspe: *Baron Munchausen*
Captain Mayne Reid: *Wilderness Home*
George Sand: *Poems*
Comtesse de Segur: *New Fairy Tales*
William Shakespeare: *Macbeth / The Tempest*
Alfred Lord Tennyson: *Idylls of the King*
Ponson du Terrail: *The Mayflower Page*

Gustave Doré was born January 6, 1832 in Strasbourg, France, just a few feet from the German border. His father was a civil engineer. The stories about Gustave's artistic childhood are legendary. His earliest known drawings are from the age of five. All those around him were dazzled by his imagination, creativity, and photographic memory. His teachers would ask him to make drawings on the blackboard to explain difficult passages to the other students. Once when he was in a parade float he did sketches of bystanders in just a few seconds and passed them out. He engraved his first lithographs (on stone) at the age of ten. He was also very theatrical.

When he was 15, his family visited Paris for the first time, and Gustave fell in love with the city. Determining to remain there, he secretly made some drawings and marched right into the office of publisher Charles Philipon. Gustave was short and looked no more than ten. Philipon did not believe that Gustave had actually made the drawings, and asked him to do more drawings on the spot. His speed and artistic quality left Philipon breathless. He sent for Gustave's father, who signed a contract making Gustave a professional illustrator. As luck would have it, Philipon was just about to launch a new humor magazine, *Journal pour Rire*. Gustave became the boy-genius cartoonist toast of Paris. The magazine's circulation soared, and by the age of 16, Gustave was the highest paid cartoonist in France, receiving 60 Francs per page. When Gustave's father died, Gustave was able to support his mother and two brothers. As a teenager, Gustave did thousands of magazine cartoons, or comic-strips.

By the early 1850s, Doré's creative genius was no longer satisfied doing cartoons, and he longed to do serious art. His first major literary illustrations were for his 1854 *Rabelais* and his 1855 *Balzac*. Those established him as one of France's premier literary illustrators. Doré became part of the cultural elite of Paris, counting among his close friends Victor Hugo, Alexandre Dumas, Theophile Gautier, and the composer Rossini. Doré did thousands of literary vignette illustrations during the 1850s, but he was still essentially a French phenomenon.

In 1861, Doré produced one of the most significant books of the 19th century. Before that, there had been two basic types of illustrations - cheap woodcut vignettes and very expensive steel engravings, usually made from paintings. Doré took the art of the people and elevated it to the level of fine art. He began a series of folio wood engravings that could almost be described as black-and-white paintings. He did 76 powerful and imaginative folio wood engravings for *Dante's Inferno*. The 13" x 17" edition weighed 20 lbs. In spite of a shocking 100 *fr* price-tag, the 3,000 copy edition sold out in weeks. With it, Doré began an extensive series of literary folios, including *Don Quixote* and *Fairy Tales*. In 1865, he did the most famous set of illustrations ever done, over 250 full-page folio engravings for *The Bible*. If people were amazed at Doré receiving 60 *fr* per illustration for his cartoons, they were shocked at the nearly 1,000 *fr* per illustration Doré received for *The Bible*. There have now been nearly 700 editions of Bibles, Bible story books, and other religious books containing those illustrations.

It was during the 1860s that Doré became the most famous artist in the world. From 1861-1900, there was a new Doré edition published every nine days! In 1864 Doré was still basically unknown in England. By 1868 he was more famous in England than any British illustrator or painter. The British discovered Doré's folios in 1865, and from 1865-68, 20 major Doré titles were published in England. It was said that Doré folios could be found in every English-speaking household where they could spell the word "art." Each new folio was a major event. They were published in 35 languages. Doré was so in demand that he trained a school of about 40 men to engrave his illustrations. It took that many people to keep up with his rate of production. Doré drew directly onto the wood block, and the engraver then painstakingly carved the illustration into the wood. That is why there is so little original Doré art. The original drawing was essentially obliterated in the carving process. A high-quality first edition of a Doré folio is as close as you can get to original art. When they first came out, Doré folios were very expensive. The first American edition (1867) of the *Doré Bible* sold for $64-$150, the deluxe version costing about a year's wages. The common people had to wait a generation to afford Doré editions.

But Doré again became restless, and the success of his folio illustrations gradually brought him less and less fulfillment. He turned to oil painting, then watercolor landscapes, then etchings, then sculpture. Doré had a major problem with the French fine art establishment. They would not accept him, because they considered him to be a renegade who somehow became wealthy and famous without paying his dues within the establishment. But the British accepted him as both illustrator and painter. A collection of his paintings was set up in London, called The Doré Gallery. It was open continuously from 1869-1892. The most popular of Doré's paintings were large religious scenes, some 20 feet high by 30 feet wide. Several of those were made into 22" x 33" steel engravings, which sold at the gallery. His Bible engravings and religious paintings earned him the title of "Painter-Preacher" in the 1870s. But the 1870s were a bitter decade for Doré personally - the Franco-Prussian War, the deaths of many of his older friends, and unhappy romances. His legions of fans knew almost nothing of his unhappiness, seeing him only as a famous, successful illustrator. Many of his personal problems were due to his emotional overdependence on his mother, whom he barely outlived. He never married or had any children. He died January 23, 1883 of a massive stroke.

In America, Doré's popularity actually increased after his death, where hundreds of cheaper "pirate" editions of his folios made them available to lower economic classes. Doré folios that sold for $50 in the 1860s sold for as low as $5 in the 1880s. In the 1890s, The Doré Gallery finally toured America. It came as far west as Chicago in 1896, where 13 years after his death, he was finally vindicated as a painter, when his display broke every attendance record in the history of the Art Institute of Chicago, all of which still stand. Attendance topped 16,000 in one day, and 4,000 in one hour. In eight months, 1.5 million people viewed the exhibit. His paintings had technical imperfections (particularly color), but they were very powerful and imaginative. His paintings were like large color illustrations and his illustrations were like b&w paintings. There is still a steady flow of Doré editions published around the world today. But there had never been a major English-language reference work on Doré until my recent book, *Gustave Doré - Adrift on Dreams of Splendor*.

Chronological List of First Book Editions of Doré Titles

year	illos	author: title
1847	105	**Doré:** *The Toils of Hercules*
1851	155	**Doré:** *Three Malcontent Artists*
	175	**Doré:** *An Unpleasant Pleasure Trip*
1852	134	**Lacroix:** *Bibliophile Jacob*
	19	**Brot:** *Alone in the World*
1853	24	**Byron:** *Complete Works*
1854	6	**Brot:** *The King's Executioner*
	10	**Brot:** *Doctor of the Heart*
	500	**Doré:** *The History of Holy Russia*
	105	**Rabelais:** *Gargantua & Pantagruel*
	20	**Doré:** *The People of Paris*
	24	**Doré:** *Parisian Menagerie*
1855	11	**Gerard:** *The Lion Hunter*
	30	**Sherer:** *Gold Prospectors*
	425	**Balzac:** *Droll Stories*
	64	**Taine:** *Mineral Waters of the Pyrenees*
	11	*The War in the Orient (Crimea)*
1856	13	*The Legend of the Wandering Jew*
	12	**Dumas:** *The Duke of Savoy's Page*
	30	**Gastineau:** *The French in Africa*
	14	**Girardin:** *Tales of an Old Maid*
	8	**Haussmann:** *Insurrection in China*
	20	**Lafon:** *Jaufre the Knight*
	9	**Noir:** *The Bronze Man*
	24	**Reid:** *Wilderness Home*
	48	**Perceval:** *Memories of a Young Cadet*
	12	**Plouvier:** *Sabbath Choruses*
1857	12	**Lafon:** *National Legends*
	20	**Segur:** *New Fairy Tales*
1858	8	**Dumas:** *Jehu's Companions*
1859	20	**Doré:** *Gallic Follies*
	31	*The War in Italy*
	20	*Battle for Italian Independence*
	324	**Malte-Brun:** *Worldwide Geography*
	12	**Montaigne:** *Essays*
1860	137	**LaBedolliere:** *Modern Paris*
	271	**Taine:** *The Pyrenees* (see 1855)
	5	**Shakespeare:** *The Tempest*
1861	29	**Aimard:** *A Ball of Francs*
	158	**About:** *King of the Mountains*
	76	**Dante:** *The Inferno*
	52	**Dumas:** *Complete Works*
	6	*Garibaldi & the Italian Volunteers*
	34	**deKock:** *Monsieur Dupont*
	12	**Malo:** *Songs of Yesteryear*
	203	**Saintine:** *The Pathway of Children*

year	illos	author: title
1862	12	*The Album of Gustave Doré*
	31	**Laujon:** *Tales & Legends*
	42	**Perrault:** *Fairy Tales*
	36	**Ainsworth:** *All Round the World*
	158	**Raspe:** *Baron Munchausen*
	165	**Saintine:** *Mythology of the Rhine*
	42	**L'Epine:** *Captain Castagnette*
1863	24	*History of France*
	44	**Chateaubriand:** *Atala*
	377	**Cervantes:** *Don Quixote*
	177	**L'Epine:** *Croque-Mitaine*
	9	**Segur:** *New Fairy Tales* (see 1857)
1864	11	**Marx:** *One Minute Story*
1865	20	*Sinbad (Arabian Nights)*
	4	**Moore:** *The Epicurean*
1866	60	**Gautier:** *Captain Fracasse*
	50	**Milton:** *Paradise Lost*
	228	*The Holy Bible*
	37	*The Holy Bible* (2nd ed)
1867	303	**Doré:** *200 Sketches*
	2	**Hugo:** *Toilers of the Sea*
	334	**LaFontaine:** *Fables*
	11	**Terrail:** *The Mayflower Page*
1868	60	**Dante:** *Purgatory & Paradise*
	21	**LaFontaine:** *Fables* (see 1867)
	37	**Tennyson:** *Idylls of the King*
1869	6	**Feval:** *Gold Prospectors*
	7	**Lamothe:** *Martyrs of Siberia*
1870	9	**Hood:** *Poems*
	10	**L'Epine:** *Knight Good-Times*
	34	**Manning:** *Spanish Pictures*
1871	5	**Jerrold:** *The Cockaynes in Paris*
1872	180	**Jerrold:** *London, a Pilgrimage*
1873	13	**Lachatre:** *History of the Popes*
	614	**Rabelais:** *Works* (see 1854)
1874	306	**Davillier:** *Spain*
1876	42	**Coleridge:** *Rime of the Ancient Mariner*
1877	100	**Michaud:** *History of the Crusades*
1879	46	**Ferry:** *The Forest Ranger*
	618	**Ariosto:** *Orlando Furioso*
1883	26	**Poe:** *The Raven*
	19	*Society of French Watercolorists*
1893	25	*The Doré Gallery: Illustrated Catalogue*
1907	95	**Doré:** *Versailles & Paris in 1871*

new illos in reprint eds: Rabelais (1854+73) Taine (1855+60)
Segur (1857+63) Bible (1866:1st+2nd) LaFntn. (1867+68)

The Mystery of the Doré Folio Cover, by Dan Malan

The Doré folio of *Poe's The Raven* was published in December of 1883, and for over a century it contained a major mystery. Doré died in January of 1883, just after completing the *Raven* illustrations, so he was not able to supervise the American engravers of the wood blocks. This was the only Doré folio commissioned by an American publisher, and Harper & Bros. then hired well-known American artist Elihu Vedder to do the title-page illustration showing Poe and Doré facing each other. The mystery was the cover illustration, clearly ahead of its time, a stylized art nouveau drawing with enough gold on the angel's wings to blind you. It was by far the largest illustration in the book. The Doré engravings averaged about 9½" x 12½" but the cover illustration filled the 14½" x 18½" cloth binding. In the lower right corner of the cover, the artist's initials "D.W." were clearly visible. While the title-page identified Doré and Vedder, it did not mention the cover artist. Near the end of Edmund C. Stedman's introduction, he mentions the cover artist only as "an American woman." There is one little problem with that. In 1883, there were no American woman book illustrators! There was a surge in American female illustrators in the early part of this century, but most of those came from Howard Pyle's famous school which began in the 1890s. There were a couple female British illustrators a generation earlier, but in 1883 American book illustration was still a male domain.

The identity of "D.W. - an American woman" remained a mystery until 1993. Even Pollin's comprehensive reference work on Poe illustrations in 1989 was unable to identify her. As this writer was doing research for the Doré book, I became intrigued by this mystery woman, but all of the leads resulted in dead ends. Years went by, till I discovered her identity by accident. The reason no one could find her was because she was not a book illustrator. In fact, of all the references to her and her works, not one of them even mentions her doing the cover to the Doré *Raven* folio. She never really sought fame, but she was briefly famous in the early American arts & crafts movement. Her name was **DORA WHEELER** (1856-1940).

Dora's artistic career lasted about a decade, and was largely controlled by three people: her mother Candace Wheeler, her art teacher William Merrit Chase, and her early mentor, Louis Prang. Candace Wheeler (1828-1923) was the proverbial domineering mother. Candace wrote her final book at the age of 93. Dora was 67 when her mother died, and by then had lost all interest in art. Dora was artistically talented as a child, but her art career began when her mother saw the British arts & crafts exhibit at the 1876 U.S. centennial. That motivated Candace to start a U.S. branch of the arts & crafts movement, which came to include the likes of Louis Comfort Tiffany and Elizabeth Custer. Candace has now come to be regarded as an early feminist. In 1878, Candace determined that Dora should get art training just like any man, and not just in the more domestic arts & crafts. So Dora began taking art lessons from William Merrit Chase, just returned from Europe. From 1880-1884, Louis Prang held annual Christmas card design contests, with a top prize of $2000. Dora won 2nd

place in 1881, and then the top prize in 1882. That 1882 design is shown here. Although it is not as sophisticated as the Doré folio cover, notice the similarities: angels with pointed chins and short curly hair holding lighted candles, and (though it is difficult to see in this b&w reduction) those same "D.W." initials in the lower right corner. And guess who finished second in that 1882 contest? Elihu Vedder. The Harper people (after Doré's untimely death) possibly wanted to add some American art flavor to this American classic illustrated by a Frenchman. Someone came across those 1882 Christmas cards from the contest, and asserted that with a few alterations, one of those angels would be ideal for the Doré folio cover. Here is how Stedman described the cover: *An American woman has wrought the image of a star-eyed Genius with the final torch, the exquisite semblance of one whose vision beholds, but whose lips may not utter, the mysteries of a land beyond "the door of a legended tomb."*

Dora's artistic career had three brief stages: Christmas cards (early 1880s), tapestries for her mother's business (mid-1880s), and painting portraits of famous acquaintances of her mother (late 1880s). In the 1890s, she did do a few magazine illustrations and a ceiling mural for one of the Columbus exposition buildings (arranged by her mother), but her artistic career was basically over. She married Boudinot Keith (taking his name) and had a family. But Dora had another claim to fame. Back in 1883, William Merritt Chase painted *Portrait of Miss Dora Wheeler* which won major exhibition awards, hailed as showing "a new generation of independent women artists." The only problem was that the face did not really look like Dora at all. Evidently Dora's face was not exotic enough. A generation later, Dora's own daughter wanted to repaint that face. In 1922, Dora donated the painting to the Cleveland Museum of Art, and there is a major article on Dora by Karal Ann Marling in their February 1978 bulletin. Dora Wheeler could be described as a talented but passive person who wanted serenity more than fame and fortune.

Illustrated Editions of *The Raven*, by Dan Malan

Note: for information about illustrated editions of Poe, see **Burton Pollin**: *Images of Poe's Works*, Greenwood Press, Westport, CT ©1989

To understand the illustrated editions to *Poe's The Raven*, which was first published in 1845, you have to go back another century or so. In the 18th century, very few first editions ever had illustrations. Works as famous as Shakespeare were not illustrated for over a century after they first came out. Other favorite 18th century illustrated titles included *Don Quixote* and *Aesop's Fables*. Only after titles were well established as classics did publishers take a chance on the great expense of engravings. What we think of as photographic reproduction did not come into vogue until nearly the end of the 19th century. Before that, any illustration had to be laboriously carved as an engraving on stone, steel, copper, or wood, and publishers would not take that risk on new titles. But along came Charles Dickens in the 1830s and changed all that. His works quickly became very popular, and he capitalized on that by issuing new titles in monthly paper parts; each month you got one chapter and two engravings. France was also well advanced in book illustration at that time, but America lagged far behind, and would not really catch up until after the Civil War.

So even though *The Raven* was very well received in 1845, there was no thought of illustrating it. When the first British edition came out in 1846, Dante Gabriel Rossetti thought *The Raven* was fantastic, and made some illustrations for it, but they were not then published in any book edition. In 1853 a British edition contained one small illustration by E.H.Wehnert, but it was not particularly significant. It was 1858 before the first significant illustrations for *The Raven* were published; four in England by Sir John Tenniel (of *Alice in Wonderland* fame) and one in the U.S. by Felix Darley (America's first great illustrator). There were a few more illustrations in the 1860s by David Scattergood and C.J.Staniland. In the 30 years after the 1st edition of *The Raven*, only a dozen illustrations were published, all by U.S. or British illustrators. Many publishers were waiting for the copyright to expire at the end of 1883.

Poe's French popularity is shown by the two Frenchmen who produced what are now considered the two greatest sets of *Raven* illustrations. In 1875, Edouard Manet did five lithographs for an enormous French *Raven* folio. My only complaint about that edition is that if they were going to publish such an edition, why did they not do more lithographs? As 1883 neared, U.S. publisher Harper commissioned Gustave Doré to do 26 folio *Raven* engravings. The Manet and Doré folios are prized collector's editions. The Poe Museum in Richmond, Virginia has a set of the Doré engravings on display, where I recently gave a series of talks. Harper's magazine announced the Doré *Raven* folio in September of 1883. It was published that December, in a red and blue gift box, and sold for $10. It was a bargain compared to other Doré folios a decade earlier, which sold for $20-$50.

While Harper was dealing with Doré, a poor British artist named James Carling submitted about 40 *Raven* illustrations to Harper, trying to get the commission. He did not succeed, and died a pauper in 1887. His illustrations were resurrected in the 1930s, and finally published in book form in 1982 by Roscoe Brown Fisher. The original illustrations are on display, and the book is for sale at the Poe Museum in Richmond. Also published at the end of 1883 was a smaller *Raven* edition with 17 William Ladd Taylor vignettes. After that, *Raven* illustrations slowed to a trickle: six by Harry Edwards (1895), two by W.Heath Robinson (1900), one by Charles Copeland in the famous set of Poe's works (1902), two by Frederick Simpson Coburn (1902), two by Edmund Dulac (1909), and ten by John R. Neill (1910). Two recent sets of illustrations deserve some notice. In 1954, **MAD**#9 (then a comic, before it was a magazine) published a brilliant *Raven* satire with 45 art panels by Bill Elder. What I especially enjoy about it is that they did not change one word of Poe's text. All of the satire is achieved by the illustrations. In 1990, *Classics Illustrated* #1 (a new version of the old 1940s-1960s series) features seven Gahan Wilson *Raven* illustrations. Though this is officially a "comic-book" series, this adaptation uses neither word balloons nor sequential art panels, and is very similar to 19th century engravings.

Top Row: **Tenniel** (1858), **Scattergood** (1865).   Bottom Row: **Manet**-2 (1875)   **9**

Top Row: **Taylor** (1883), **Dulac**-inset (1909), **Carling** (1883-unpublished)
Bottom Row: **Edwards** (1895), **Robinson**-2 (1900)

Top Row: **Copeland** (1902), **Coburn**-2 (1902)
Bottom Row: **Elder** (©1954 MAD Comics/William Gaines)
Wilson (© 1990 Berkley/First Publishing)

THE RAVEN

BY

EDGAR ALLAN POE

ILLUSTRATED

BY GUSTAVE DORÉ

WITH COMMENT BY EDMUND C. STEDMAN

NEW YORK

HARPER & BROTHERS, PUBLISHERS, FRANKLIN SQUARE

1884

COMMENT ON THE POEM.

THE secret of a poem, no less than a jest's prosperity, lies in the ear of him that hears it. Yield to its spell, accept the poet's mood: this, after all, is what the sages answer when you ask them of its value. Even though the poet himself, in his other mood, tell you that his art is but sleight of hand, his food enchanter's food, and offer to show you the trick of it,—believe him not. Wait for his prophetic hour; then give yourself to his passion, his joy or pain. "We are in Love's hand to-day!" sings Gautier, in Swinburne's buoyant paraphrase,—and from morn to sunset we are wafted on the violet sea: there is but one love, one May, one flowery strand. Love is eternal, all else unreal and put aside. The vision has an end, the scene changes; but we have gained something, the memory of a charm. As many poets, so many charms. There is the charm of Evanescence, that which lends to supreme beauty and grace an aureole of Pathos. Share with Landor his one "night of memories and of sighs" for Rose Aylmer, and you have this to the full.

And now take the hand of a new-world minstrel, strayed from some proper habitat to that rude and dissonant America which, as Baudelaire saw, "was for Poe only a vast prison through which he ran, hither and thither, with the feverish agitation of a being created to breathe in a purer world," and where "his interior life, spiritual as a poet, spiritual even as a drunkard, was but one perpetual effort to escape the influence of this antipathetical atmosphere." Clasp the sensitive hand of a troubled singer dreeing thus his weird, and share with him the clime in which he found,—never throughout the day, always in the night,—if not the Atlantis whence he had wandered, at least a place of refuge from the bounds in which by day he was immured.

To one land only he has power to lead you, and for one night only can you share his dream. A tract of neither Earth nor Heaven: "No-man's-land," out of Space, out of Time. Here are the perturbed ones, through whose eyes, like those of the Cenci, the soul finds windows though the mind is dazed; here spirits, groping for the path which leads to Eternity, are halted and delayed. It is the limbo of "planetary souls," wherein are all moonlight uncertainties, all lost loves and illusions. Here some are fixed in trance, the only respite attainable; others

> "move fantastically
> To a discordant melody:"

while everywhere are

> "Sheeted Memories of the Past—
> Shrouded forms that start and sigh
> As they pass the wanderer by."

Such is the land, and for one night we enter it,—a night of astral phases and recurrent chimes. Its monodies are twelve poems, whose music strives to change yet ever is the same. One by one they sound, like the chiming of the brazen and ebony clock, in "The Masque of the Red Death," which made the waltzers pause with "disconcert and tremulousness and meditation," as often as the hour came round.

Of all these mystical cadences, the plaint of *The Raven*, vibrating through the portal, chiefly has impressed the outer world. What things go to the making of a poem,—and how true in this, as in most else, that race which named its bards "the makers"! A work is called out of the void. Where there was nothing, it remains,—a new creation, part of the treasure of mankind. And a few exceptional lyrics, more than others that are equally creative, compel us to think anew how bravely the poet's pen turns things unknown

> "to shapes, and gives to airy nothing
> A local habitation, and a name."

Each seems without a prototype, yet all fascinate us with elements wrested from the shadow of the Supernatural. Now the highest imagination is concerned about the soul of things; it may or may not inspire the Fantasy that peoples with images the interlunar vague. Still, one of these lyrics, in its smaller way, affects us with a sense of uniqueness, as surely as the sublimer works of a supernatural cast,—Marlowe's "Faustus," the "Faust" of Goethe, "Manfred," or even those ethereal masterpieces, "The Tempest" and "A Midsummer Night's Dream." More than one, while otherwise unique, has some burden or refrain which haunts the memory,—once heard, never forgotten, like the tone of a rarely used but distinctive organ-stop. Notable among them is Bürger's "Lenore," that ghostly and resonant ballad, the lure and foil of the translators. Few will deny that Coleridge's wondrous "Rime of the Ancient Mariner" stands at their very head. "Le Juif-Errant" would have claims, had Beranger been a greater poet; and, but for their remoteness from popular sympathy, "The Lady of Shalott" and "The Blessed Damozel" might be added to the list. It was given to Edgar Allan Poe to produce two lyrics, "The Bells" and *The Raven*, each of which, although perhaps of less beauty than those of Tennyson and Rossetti, is a unique. "Ulalume," while equally strange and imaginative, has not the universal quality that is a portion of our test.

The Raven in sheer poetical constituents falls below such pieces as "The Haunted Palace," "The City in the Sea," "The Sleeper," and "Israfel." The whole of it would be exchanged, I suspect, by readers of a fastidious cast, for such passages as these:

> "Around, by lifting winds forgot,
> Resignedly beneath the sky
> The melancholy waters lie.
>
> No rays from the holy heaven come down
> On the long night-time of that town;
> But light from out the lurid sea
> Streams up the turrets silently—
> * * * * * * *
> Up many and many a marvellous shrine
> Whose wreathéd friezes intertwine
> The viol, the violet, and the vine.
> * * * * * * *
> No swellings tell that winds may be
> Upon some far-off happier sea—
> No heavings hint that winds have been
> On seas less hideously serene."

It lacks the aerial melody of the poet whose heart-strings are a lute:

> "And they say (the starry choir
>   And the other listening things)
> That Israfeli's fire
> Is owing to that lyre
>   By which he sits and sings—
> The trembling living wire
> Of those unusual strings."

But *The Raven*, like "The Bells" and "Annabel Lee," commends itself to the many and the few. I have said elsewhere that Poe's rarer productions seemed to me "those in which there is the appearance, at least, of spontaneity,—in which he yields to his feelings, while dying falls and cadences most musical, most melancholy, come from him una-

wares." This is still my belief; and yet, upon a fresh study of this poem, it impresses me more than at any time since my boyhood. Close acquaintance tells in favor of every true work of art. Induce the man, who neither knows art nor cares for it, to examine some poem or painting, and how soon its force takes hold of him! In fact, he will overrate the relative value of the first good work by which his attention has been fairly caught. *The Raven*, also, has consistent qualities which even an expert must admire. In no other of its author's poems is the motive more palpably defined. "The Haunted Palace" is just as definite to the select reader, but Poe scarcely would have taken that subtle allegory for bald analysis. *The Raven* is wholly occupied with the author's typical theme—the irretrievable loss of an idolized and beautiful woman; but on other grounds, also, the public instinct is correct in thinking it his representative poem.

A man of genius usually gains a footing with the success of some one effort, and this not always his greatest. Recognition is the more instant for having been postponed. He does not acquire it, like a miser's fortune, coin after coin, but "not at all or all in all." And thus with other ambitions: the courtier, soldier, actor,—whatever their parts,—each counts his triumph from some lucky stroke. Poe's Raven, despite augury, was for him "the bird that made the breeze to blow." The poet settled in New-York, in the winter of 1844-'45, finding work upon Willis's paper, "The Evening Mirror," and eking out his income by contributions elsewhere. For six years he had been an active writer, and enjoyed a professional reputation; was held in both respect and misdoubt, and was at no loss for his share of the ill-paid journalism of that day. He also had done much of his very best work,—such tales as "Ligeia" and "The Fall of the House of Usher," (the latter containing that mystical counterpart, in verse, of Elihu Vedder's "A Lost Mind,") such analytic feats as "The Gold Bug" and "The Mystery of Marie Roget." He had made proselytes abroad, and gained a lasting hold upon the French mind. He had learned his own power and weakness, and was at his prime, and not without a certain reputation. But he had written nothing that was on the tongue of everybody. To rare and delicate work some popular touch must be added to capture the general audience of one's own time.

Through the industry of Poe's successive biographers, the hit made by *The Raven* has become an oft-told tale. The poet's young wife, Virginia, was fading before his eyes, but lingered for another year within death's shadow. The long, low chamber in the house near the Bloomingdale Road is as famous as the room where Rouget de l'Isle composed the Marseillaise. All have heard that the poem, signed "Quarles," appeared in the "American Review," with a pseudo-editorial comment on its form; that Poe received ten dollars for it; that Willis, the kindest and least envious of fashionable arbiters, reprinted it with a eulogy that instantly made it the town-talk. All doubt of its authorship was dispelled when Poe recited it himself at a literary gathering, and for a time he was the most marked of American authors. The hit stimulated and encouraged him. Like another and prouder satirist, he too found "something of summer" even "in the hum of insects." Sorrowfully enough, but three years elapsed,—a period of influence, pride, anguish, yet always of imaginative or critical labor,— before the final defeat, before the curtain dropped on a life that for him was in truth a tragedy, and he yielded to "the Conqueror Worm."

"The American Review: A Whig Journal" was a creditable magazine for the time, double-columned, printed on good paper with clear type, and illustrated by mezzotint portraits. Amid much matter below the present standard, it contained some that any editor would be glad to receive. The initial volume, for 1845, has articles by Horace Greeley, Donald Mitchell, Walter Whitman, Marsh, Tuckerman, and Whipple. Ralph Hoyt's quaint poem, "Old," appeared in this volume. And here are three lyrics by Poe: "The City in the Sea," "The Valley of Unrest," and *The Raven*. Two of these were built up,—such was his way,—from earlier studies, but the last-named came out as if freshly composed, and almost as we have it now. The statement that it was not afterward revised is erroneous. Eleven trifling changes from the magazine-text appear in *The Raven and Other Poems*, 1845, a book which the poet shortly felt encouraged to offer the public. These are mostly changes of punctuation, or of single words, the latter kind made to heighten the effect of alliteration. In Mr. Lang's pretty edition of Poe's verse, brought out in the "Parchment Library," he has shown the instinct of a scholar, and has done wisely, in going back to the text of the volume just mentioned, as given in the London issue of 1846. The "standard" Griswold collection of the poet's works abounds with errors. These have been repeated by later editors, who also have made new errors of their own. But the text of *The Raven*, owing to the requests made to the author for manuscript copies, was still farther revised by him; in fact, he printed it in Richmond, just before his death, with the poetic substitution of "seraphim whose foot-falls" for "angels whose faint foot-falls," in the fourteenth stanza. Our present text, therefore, while substan-

tially that of 1845, is somewhat modified by the poet's later reading, and is, I think, the most correct and effective version of this single poem. The most radical change from the earliest version appeared, however, in the volume of 1845; the eleventh stanza originally having contained these lines, faulty in rhyme and otherwise a blemish on the poem:

"Caught from some unhappy master, whom unmerciful
    Disaster
Followed fast and followed faster—so, when Hope he
    would adjure,
Stern Despair returned, instead of the sweet Hope he
    dared adjure—
        That sad answer, 'Nevermore!'"

It would be well if other, and famous, poets could be as sure of making their changes always improvements. Poe constantly rehandled his scanty show of verse, and usually bettered it. *The Raven* was the first of the few poems which he nearly brought to completion before printing. It may be that those who care for poetry lost little by his death. Fluent in prose, he never wrote verse for the sake of making a poem. When a refrain or image haunted him, the lyric that resulted was the inspiration, as he himself said, of a passion, not of a purpose. This was at intervals so rare as almost to justify the Fairfield theory that each was the product of a nervous crisis.

What, then, gave the poet his clue to *The Raven?* From what misty foundation did it rise slowly to a music slowly breathed? As usual, more than one thing went to the building of so notable a poem. Considering the longer sermons often preached on brief and less suggestive texts, I hope not to be blamed for this discussion of a single lyric,—especially one which an artist like Doré has made the subject of prodigal illustration. Until recently I had supposed that this piece, and a few which its author composed after its appearance, were exceptional in not having grown from germs in his boyish verse. But Mr. Fearing Gill has shown me some unpublished stanzas by Poe, written in his eighteenth year, and entitled "The Demon of the Fire." The manuscript appears to be in the poet's early handwriting, and its genuineness is vouched for by the family in whose possession it has remained for half a century. Besides the plainest germs of "The Bells" and "The Haunted Palace" it contains a few lines somewhat suggestive of the opening and close of *The Raven*. As to the rhythm of our poem, a comparison of dates indicates that this was influenced by the rhythm of "Lady Geraldine's Courtship." Poe was one of the first to honor Miss Barrett's genius; he inscribed his collected poems to her as "the noblest of her sex," and was in sympathy with her lyrical method. The lines from her love-poem,

"With a murmurous stir uncertain, in the air, the purple curtain
Swelleth in and swelleth out around her motionless pale
    brows,"

found an echo in these:

"And the silken sad uncertain rustling of each purple curtain
Thrilled me—filled me with fantastic terrors never felt before."

Here Poe assumed a privilege for which he roughly censured Longfellow, and which no one ever sought on his own premises without swift detection and chastisement. In melody and stanzaic form, we shall see that the two poems are not unlike, but in motive they are totally distinct. The generous poetess felt nothing but the true originality of the poet. "This vivid writing!" she exclaimed,—"this power which is felt! . . . . Our great poet, Mr. Browning, author of 'Paracelsus,' &c., is enthusiastic in his admiration of the rhythm." Mr. Ingram, after referring to "Lady Geraldine," cleverly points out another source from which Poe may have caught an impulse. In 1843, Albert Pike, the half-Greek, half-frontiersman, poet of Arkansas, had printed in "The New Mirror," for which Poe then was writing, some verses entitled "Isadore," but since revised by the author and called "The Widowed Heart." I select from Mr. Pike's revision the following stanza, of which the main features correspond with the original version:

"Restless I pace our lonely rooms, I play our songs no more,
The garish sun shines flauntingly upon the unswept floor;
The mocking-bird still sits and sings, O melancholy strain!
For my heart is like an autumn-cloud that overflows with rain;
    Thou art lost to me forever, Isadore!"

Here we have a prolonged measure, a similarity of refrain, and the introduction of a bird whose song enhances sorrow. There are other trails which may be followed by the curious; notably, a passage which Mr. Ingram selects from Poe's final review of "Barnaby Rudge":

'The raven, too, * * * might have been made, more than we now see it, a portion of the conception of the fantastic Barnaby. * * * Its character might have performed, in regard to that of the idiot, much the same part as does, in music, the accompaniment in respect to the air.'

Nevertheless, after pointing out these germs and resemblances, the value of this poem still is found in its originality. The progressive music, the scenic detail and contrasted light and shade,—above all, the spiritual passion of the nocturn, make it the work of an informing genius. As for the gruesome

bird, he is unlike all other ravens of his clan, from the "twa corbies" and "three ravens" of the balladists to Barnaby's rumpled "Grip." Here is no semblance of the cawing rook that haunts ancestral turrets and treads the field of heraldry; no boding phantom of which Tickell sang that, when,

"shrieking at her window thrice,
    The raven flap'd his wing,
Too well the love-lorn maiden knew
    The solemn boding sound."

Poe's raven is a distinct conception; the incarnation of a mourner's agony and hopelessness; a sable embodied Memory, the abiding chronicler of doom, a type of the Irreparable. Escaped across the Styx, from "the Night's Plutonian shore," he seems the imaged soul of the questioner himself,—of him who can not, will not, quaff the kind nepenthe, because the memory of Lenore is all that is left him, and with the surcease of his sorrow even that would be put aside.

The Raven also may be taken as a representative poem of its author, for its exemplification of all his notions of what a poem should be. These are found in his essays on "The Poetic Principle," "The Rationale of Verse," and "The Philosophy of Composition." Poe declared that "in Music, perhaps, the soul most nearly attains the great end for which, when inspired by the Poetic Sentiment, it struggles —the creation of supernal Beauty. . . . Verse cannot be better designated than as an inferior or less capable music"; but again, verse which is really the "Poetry of Words" is "The Rhythmical Creation of Beauty,"—this and nothing more. The *tone* of the highest Beauty is one of Sadness. The most melancholy of topics is Death. This must be allied to Beauty. "The death, then, of a beautiful woman is, unquestionably, the most poetical topic in the world,—and equally is it beyond doubt that the lips best suited for such a topic are those of a bereaved lover." These last expressions are quoted from Poe's whimsical analysis of this very poem, but they indicate precisely the general range of his verse. The climax of "The Bells" is the muffled monotone of ghouls, who glory in weighing down the human heart. "Lenore," *The Raven*, "The Sleeper," "To One in Paradise," and "Ulalume" form a tenebrose symphony,—and "Annabel Lee," written last of all, shows that one theme possessed him to the end. Again, these are all nothing if not musical, and some are touched with that quality of the Fantastic which awakes the sense of awe, and adds a new fear to agony itself. Through all is dimly outlined, beneath a shadowy pall, the poet's ideal love,—so often half-portrayed elsewhere, —the entombed wife of Usher, the Lady Ligeia, in truth the counterpart of his own nature. I suppose that an artist's love for one "in the form" never can wholly rival his devotion to some ideal. The woman near him must exercise her spells, be all by turns and nothing long, charm him with infinite variety, or be content to forego a share of his allegiance. He must be lured by the Unattainable, and this is ever just beyond him in his passion for creative art.

Poe, like Hawthorne, came in with the decline of the Romantic school, and none delighted more than he to laugh at its calamity. Yet his heart was with the romancers and their Oriental or Gothic effects. His invention, so rich in the prose tales, seemed to desert him when he wrote verse; and his judgment told him that long romantic poems depend more upon incident than inspiration,—and that, to utter the poetry of romance, lyrics would suffice. Hence his theory, clearly fitted to his own limitations, that "a 'long poem' is a flat contradiction in terms." The components of *The Raven* are few and simple: a man, a bird, and the phantasmal memory of a woman. But the piece affords a fine display of romantic material. What have we? The midnight; the shadowy chamber with its tomes of forgotten lore; the student,—a modern Hieronymus; the raven's tap on the casement; the wintry night and dying fire; the silken wind-swept hangings; the dreams and vague mistrust of the echoing darkness; the black, uncanny bird upon the pallid bust; the accessories of violet velvet and the gloating lamp. All this stage effect of situation, light, color, sound, is purely romantic, and even melodramatic, but of a poetic quality that melodrama rarely exhibits, and thoroughly reflective of the poet's "eternal passion, eternal pain."

The rhythmical structure of *The Raven* was sure to make an impression. Rhyme, alliteration, the burden, the stanzaic form, were devised with singular adroitness. Doubtless the poet was struck with the aptness of Miss Barrett's musical trochaics, in "eights," and especially by the arrangement adopted near the close of "Lady Geraldine":

"'Eyes,' he said, 'now throbbing through me! Are ye eyes
    that did undo me?
Shining eyes, like antique jewels set in Parian statue-stone!
Underneath that calm white forehead, are ye ever burning
    torrid
O'er the desolate sand-desert of my heart and life undone?'"

His artistic introduction of a third rhyme in both the second and fourth lines, and the addition of a fifth line and a final refrain, made the stanza of *The Raven*. The persistent alliteration seems to come without effort, and often the rhymes within lines are seductive; while the refrain or burden dominates the whole work. Here also he had profited by Miss Barrett's study of ballads and romaunts in her own and other tongues. A "refrain" is the lure wherewith a poet or a musician holds the wandering ear, —the recurrent longing of Nature for the initial strain. I have always admired the beautiful refrains of the English songstress,—"The Nightingales, the Nightingales," "Margret, Margret," "My Heart and I," "Toll slowly," "The River floweth on," "Pan, Pan is dead," etc. She also employed what I term the Repetend, in the use of which Poe has excelled all poets since Coleridge thus revived it:

"O happy living things! no tongue
    Their beauty might declare:
A spring of love gushed from my heart,
    And I blessed them unaware:
Sure my kind saint took pity on me,
    And I blessed them unaware."

Poe created the fifth line of his stanza for the magic of the repetend. He relied upon it to the uttermost in a few later poems,—"Lenore," "Annabel Lee," "Ulalume," and "For Annie." It gained a wild and melancholy music, I have thought, from the "sweet influences," of the Afric burdens and repetends that were sung to him in childhood, attuning with their native melody the voice of our Southern poet.

"The Philosophy of Composition," his analysis of *The Raven*, is a technical dissection of its method and structure. Neither his avowal of cold-blooded artifice, nor his subsequent avowal to friends that an exposure of this artifice was only another of his intellectual hoaxes, need be wholly credited. If he had designed the complete work in advance, he scarcely would have made so harsh a prelude of rattle-pan rhymes to the delicious melody of the second stanza,—not even upon his theory of the fantastic. Of course an artist, having perfected a work, sees, like the first Artist, that it is good, and sees why it is good. A subsequent analysis, coupled with a disavowal of any sacred fire, readily enough may be made. My belief is that the first conception and rough draft of this poem came as inspiration always comes; that its author then saw how it might be perfected, giving it the final touches described in his chapter on Composition, and that the latter, therefore, is neither wholly false nor wholly true. The harm of such analysis is that it tempts a novice to fancy that artificial processes can supersede imagination. The impulse of genius is to guard the secrets of its creative hour. Glimpses obtained of the toil, the baffled experiments, which precede a triumph, as in the sketch-work of Hawthorne recently brought to light, afford priceless instruction and encouragement to the sincere artist. But one who voluntarily exposes his Muse to the gaze of all comers should recall the fate of King Candaules.

The world still thinks of Poe as a "luckless man of genius." I recently heard him mentioned as "one whom everybody seems chartered to misrepresent, decry or slander." But it seems to me that his ill-luck ended with his pitiable death, and that since then his defence has been persistent, and his fame of as steadfast growth as a suffering and gifted author could pray for in his hopeful hour. Griswold's decrial and slander turned the current in his favor. Critics and biographers have come forward with successive refutations, with tributes to his character, with new editions of his works. His own letters and the minute incidents of his career are before us; the record, good and bad, is widely known. No appellor has received more tender and forgiving judgment. His mishaps in life belonged to his region and period, perchance still more to his own infirmity of will. Doubtless his environment was not one to guard a fine-grained, ill-balanced nature from perils without and within. His strongest will, to be lord of himself, gained for him "that heritage of woe." He confessed himself the bird's unhappy master, the stricken sufferer of this poem. But his was a full share of that dramatic temper which exults in the presage of its own doom. There is a delight in playing one's high part: we are all gladiators, crying *Ave Imperator!* To quote Burke's matter of fact: "In grief the pleasure is still uppermost, and the affliction we suffer has no resemblance to absolute pain, which is always odious, and which we endeavor to shake off as soon as possible." Poe went farther, and was an artist even in the tragedy of his career. If, according to his own belief, sadness and the vanishing of beauty are the highest poetic themes, and poetic feeling the keenest earthly pleasure, then the sorrow and darkness of his broken life were not without their frequent compensation.

In the following pages, we have a fresh example of an artist's genius characterizing his interpretation of a famous poem. Gustave Doré, the last work of whose pencil is before us, was not the painter, or even the draughtsman, for realists demanding truth of tone, figure, and perfection. Such matters concerned him less than to make shape and distance, light and shade, assist his purpose,—which was to excite the soul, the imagination, of the looker on. This he did by arousing our sense of awe, through marvellous and often sublime conceptions of things unutterable and full of gloom or glory. It is well said that if his works were not great paintings, as pictures they are great indeed. As a "literary artist," and such he was, his force was in direct ratio with the dramatic invention of his author, with the brave audacities of the spirit that kindled his

own. Hence his success with Rabelais, with "Le Juif-Errant," "Les Contes Drolatiques," and "Don Quixote," and hence, conversely, his failure to express the beauty of Tennyson's Idyls, of "Il Paradiso," of the Hebrew pastorals, and other texts requiring exaltation, or sweetness and repose. He was a born master of the grotesque, and by a special insight could portray the spectres of a haunted brain. We see objects as his personages saw them, and with the very eyes of the Wandering Jew, the bewildered Don, or the goldsmith's daughter whose fancy so magnifies the King in the shop on the Pont-au-Change. It was in the nature of things that he should be attracted to each masterpiece of verse or prose that I have termed unique. The lower kingdoms were called into his service; his rocks, trees and mountains, the sky itself, are animate with motive and diablerie. Had he lived to illustrate Shakespeare, we should have seen a remarkable treatment of Çaliban, the Witches, the storm in "Lear"; but doubtless should have questioned his ideals of Imogen or Miranda. Beauty pure and simple, and the perfect excellence thereof, he rarely seemed to comprehend.

Yet there is beauty in his designs for the "Ancient Mariner," unreal as they are, and a consecutiveness rare in a series by Doré. The Rime afforded him a prolonged story, with many shiftings of the scene. In *The Raven* sound and color preserve their monotone and we have no change of place or occasion. What is the result? Doré proffers a series of variations upon the theme as he conceived it, "the enigma of death and the hallucination of an inconsolable soul." In some of these drawings his faults are evident; others reveal his powerful originality, and the best qualities in which, as a draughtsman, he stood alone. Plainly there was something in common between the working moods of Poe and Doré. This would appear more clearly had the latter tried his hand upon the "Tales of the Grotesque and Arabesque." Both resorted often to the elf-land of fantasy and romance. In melodramatic feats they both, through their command of the supernatural, avoided the danger-line between the ideal and the absurd. Poe was the truer worshipper of the Beautiful; his love for it was a consecrating passion, and herein he parts company with his illustrator. Poet or artist, Death at last transfigures all: within the shadow of his sable harbinger, Vedder's symbolic crayon aptly sets them face to face, but enfolds them with the mantle of immortal wisdom and power. An American woman has wrought the image of a star-eyed Genius with the final torch, the exquisite semblance of one whose vision beholds, but whose lips may not utter, the mysteries of a land beyond "the door of a legended tomb."

EDMUND C. STEDMAN.

THE RAVEN.

ONCE upon a midnight dreary, while I pondered, weak and weary,
    Over many a quaint and curious volume of forgotten lore,—
While I nodded, nearly napping, suddenly there came a tapping,
As of some one gently rapping, rapping at my chamber door.
" 'T is some visiter," I muttered, " tapping at my chamber door—

> Only this, and nothing more."

Ah, distinctly I remember it was in the bleak December,
And each separate dying ember wrought its ghost upon the floor.
Eagerly I wished the morrow;—vainly I had sought to borrow
From my books surcease of sorrow—sorrow for the lost Lenore—
For the rare and radiant maiden whom the angels name Lenore—

> Nameless here for evermore.

And the silken sad uncertain rustling of each purple curtain
Thrilled me—filled me with fantastic terrors never felt before;
So that now, to still the beating of my heart, I stood repeating
" 'T is some visiter entreating entrance at my chamber door—
Some late visiter entreating entrance at my chamber door;—

> This it is, and nothing more."

Presently my soul grew stronger; hesitating then no longer,
"Sir," said I, "or Madam, truly your forgiveness I implore;
But the fact is I was napping, and so gently you came rapping,
And so faintly you came tapping, tapping at my chamber door,
That I scarce was sure I heard you"—here I opened wide the door;—

Darkness there, and nothing more.

Deep into that darkness peering, long I stood there wondering, fearing,
Doubting, dreaming dreams no mortal ever dared to dream before;
But the silence was unbroken, and the darkness gave no token,
And the only word there spoken was the whispered word, "Lenore!"
This I whispered, and an echo murmured back the word, "Lenore!"

Merely this and nothing more.

Back into the chamber turning, all my soul within me burning,
Soon again I heard a tapping, somewhat louder than before.
"Surely," said I, "surely that is something at my window lattice;
Let me see, then, what thereat is, and this mystery explore—
Let my heart be still a moment and this mystery explore;—

'T is the wind and nothing more!"

Open here I flung the shutter, when, with many a flirt and flutter,
In there stepped a stately Raven of the saintly days of yore.
Not the least obeisance made he; not a minute stopped or stayed he;
But, with mien of lord or lady, perched above my chamber door—
Perched upon a bust of Pallas just above my chamber door—

Perched, and sat, and nothing more.

Then this ebony bird beguiling my sad fancy into smiling,
By the grave and stern decorum of the countenance it wore,
"Though thy crest be shorn and shaven, thou," I said, "art sure no craven,
Ghastly grim and ancient Raven wandering from the Nightly shore,—
Tell me what thy lordly name is on the Night's Plutonian shore!"

> Quoth the Raven, "Nevermore."

Much I marvelled this ungainly fowl to hear discourse so plainly,
Though its answer little meaning—little relevancy bore ;
For we cannot help agreeing that no living human being
Ever yet was blessed with seeing bird above his chamber door—
Bird or beast upon the sculptured bust above his chamber door,

> With such name as "Nevermore."

But the Raven, sitting lonely on the placid bust, spoke only
That one word, as if his soul in that one word he did outpour.
Nothing further then he uttered—not a feather then he fluttered—
Till I scarcely more than muttered, "Other friends have flown before—
On the morrow *he* will leave me, as my hopes have flown before."

> Then the bird said, "Nevermore."

Startled at the stillness broken by reply so aptly spoken,
"Doubtless," said I, "what it utters is its only stock and store,
Caught from some unhappy master whom unmerciful Disaster
Followed fast and followed faster till his songs one burden bore—
Till the dirges of his Hope that melancholy burden bore

> Of ' Never—nevermore.'"

But the Raven still beguiling all my sad soul into smiling,
Straight I wheeled a cushioned seat in front of bird and bust and door;
Then, upon the velvet sinking, I betook myself to linking
Fancy unto fancy, thinking what this ominous bird of yore—
What this grim, ungainly, ghastly, gaunt, and ominous bird of yore

                        Meant in croaking "Nevermore."

This I sat engaged in guessing, but no syllable expressing
To the fowl whose fiery eyes now burned into my bosom's core;
This and more I sat divining, with my head at ease reclining
On the cushion's velvet lining that the lamplight gloated o'er,
But whose velvet violet lining with the lamplight gloating o'er

                        She shall press, ah, nevermore!

Then, methought, the air grew denser, perfumed from an unseen censer
Swung by seraphim whose foot-falls tinkled on the tufted floor.
"Wretch," I cried, "thy God hath lent thee—by these angels he hath sent thee
Respite—respite and nepenthe from thy memories of Lenore!
Quaff, oh quaff this kind nepenthe, and forget this lost Lenore!"

                        Quoth the Raven, "Nevermore."

"Prophet!" said I, "thing of evil!—prophet still, if bird or devil!—
Whether Tempter sent, or whether tempest tossed thee here ashore,
Desolate yet all undaunted, on this desert land enchanted—
On this home by Horror haunted—tell me truly, I implore—.
Is there—*is* there balm in Gilead?—tell me—tell me, I implore!"

                        Quoth the Raven, "Nevermore."

"Prophet!" said I, "thing of evil—prophet still, if bird or devil!
By that Heaven that bends above us—by that God we both adore—
Tell this soul with sorrow laden if, within the distant Aidenn,
It shall clasp a sainted maiden whom the angels name Lenore—
Clasp a rare and radiant maiden whom the angels name Lenore."

       Quoth the Raven, "Nevermore."

"Be that word our sign of parting, bird or fiend!" I shrieked, upstarting—
"Get thee back into the tempest and the Night's Plutonian shore!
Leave no black plume as a token of that lie thy soul hath spoken!
Leave my loneliness unbroken!—quit the bust above my door!
Take thy beak from out my heart, and take thy form from off my door!"

       Quoth the Raven, "Nevermore."

And the Raven, never flitting, still is sitting, still is sitting
On the pallid bust of Pallas just above my chamber door;
And his eyes have all the seeming of a demon's that is dreaming,
And the lamplight o'er him streaming throws his shadow on the floor;
And my soul from out that shadow that lies floating on the floor

       Shall be lifted—nevermore!

Plate 1: *Nevermore!*

Plate 2: *Once upon a midnight dreary, while I pondered, weak and weary,*
Over many a quaint and curious volume of forgotten lore.

Plate 3: *Ah, distinctly I remember, it was in the bleak December,*
And each separate dying ember wrought its ghost upon the floor.

Plate 4: *Eagerly I wished the morrow; vainly I had sought to borrow*
From my books surcease of sorrow - sorrow for the lost Lenore.

27

Plate 5: *Sorrow for the lost Lenore.*

Plate 6: *For the rare and radiant maiden whom the angels name Lenore -*
Nameless here for evermore.

Plate 7: *'T is some visitor entreating entrance at my chamber door -*
Some late visitor entreating entrance at my chamber door.

Plate 8: *Here I opened wide the door; Darkness there, and nothing more.*

Plate 9: *Doubting, dreaming dreams no mortal ever dared to dream before.*

Plate 10: *Surely, said I, surely that is something at my window lattice;*
Let me see, then, what thereat is, and this mystery explore

Plate 11: *Open here I flung the shutter.*

Plate 12: *A stately Raven of the saintly days of yore.*
Not the least obeisance made he; not a minute stopped or stayed he.

35

Plate 13: *Perched upon a bust of Pallas just above my chamber door -*
Perched, and sat, and nothing more.

Plate 14: *Wandering from the Nightly shore.*

Plate 15: *Till I scarcely more than muttered, Other friends have flown before -*
On the morrow he will leave me, as my hopes have flown before.

Plate 16: *Then, upon the velvet sinking, I betook myself to linking fancy unto fancy.*   39

Plate 17: *But whose velvet violet lining with the lamplight gloating o'er
She shall press, ah, nevermore!*

Plate 18: *Wretch, I cried, thy God hath lent thee - by these angels he hath sent thee*
Respite - respite and nepenthe from thy memories of Lenore!

41

Plate 19: *On this home by Horror haunted.*

Plate 20: *Tell me truly, I implore -*
Is there - is there balm in Gilead? - tell me - tell me, I implore!

Plate 21: *Tell this soul with sorrow laden if, within the distant Aidenn,*
It shall clasp a sainted maiden whom the angels name Lenore.

Plate 22: *Be that word our sign of parting, bird or fiend! I shrieked, upstarting.*

Plate 23: *Get thee back into the tempest and the Night's Plutonian shore!*

Plate 24: *And my soul from out that shadow that lies floating on the floor*
Shall be lifted - nevermore!

Ovals (2): *ΑΝΑΓΚΗ*   **and**   *The secret of the Sphinx.*